99

ALL ABOUT
HOUSE
PLANTS

ALAN TITCHMARSH

ALL ABOUT
HOUSE
PLANTS

HAMLYN

ACKNOWLEDGEMENTS

Photographs
Title page copyright BBC Enterprises
Pat Brindley, pages 21, 36, 37; George Hyde, page 57; Patrick
Johns, page 53; Photos Horticultural, page 28; The Harry
Smith Horticultural Photographic Collection, pages 15, 19,
32, 38, 40, 42, 44, 48. All other photographs by Hamlyn
Publishing.

This book is based on *Healthy House Plants* first published in 1984
by The Hamlyn Publishing Group Limited.

This revised edition published in 1986 by Hamlyn Publishing,
Bridge House, London Road, Twickenham, Middlesex, England

ISBN 0 600 30708 5

Phototypeset in England by Servis Filmsetting Limited
in 10 on 11pt Apollo

Printed in Spain by Cayfosa. Barcelona
Dep. Leg. B-11521-1986

CONTENTS

The craze for plants in the home has proved to be far more lasting than any whim of fashion

INTRODUCTION

Twenty years ago, you might have found a dozen different kinds of plants scattered around British homes. Today the figure runs into hundreds, and a wide choice of plants means that it will be easier for you to pick the kind of plant that can survive and grow well in your conditions. It's all very well to say that a plant needs 'a temperature between 10 and 16°C (50 and 60°F),' but if that means you have to turn your centrally-heated haven into an igloo it won't cut much ice. If you see what I mean. No; choose well at the outset and you'll both be able to live in harmony.

The only problem with introducing plants into the home, is that there's a temptation to treat them like bits of furniture. Resist the temptation and treat them rather more like a dog or a cat. However, over-cossetting can also lead to problems. More house plants die of being overwatered than anything else. They don't require daily ministrations when the hand of the clock is on twelve; instead they need more observation on your part so that they can be fed and watered when they are hungry and thirsty, and this depends on the time of year and the weather conditions.

We still lag miles behind other European countries when it comes to the skills needed for growing house plants. Take a trip to Holland and you'll hardly be able to see into any houses thanks to a forest of amazingly vigorous growth on the inside windowsills.

But there are short cuts. This little book is one of them. By the time you get to the end of it you'll realise that one thing more than any other is responsible for growing better plants than before. It's called common sense – a sort of hybrid between what you can see the plant needs and what you feel about it in your bones. It's sometimes known as green fingers, but it's really a matter of finding out the kind of conditions a plant is happiest growing in, and then doing your level best to provide them.

And house plants do have one advantage over dogs and cats: they need very little exercise!

FINDING A HEALTHY PLANT

A house plant that's bristling with health and full of energy when you buy it will give you a head start when it comes to keeping it happy at home, so it makes sense to shop around for the best.

You'll find house plants on sale in all sorts of places, but here's a list of where to buy them, given in order of preference:

- The nursery where the plant was grown
- A garden centre
- A chain store or supermarket
- A greengrocer's shop

The idea is to get the plant home with as little shock to its system as possible. Buy from a nursery or garden centre and the plant will have been well cared for and is unlikely to have caught a chill.

Buy from a supermarket or chain store only if the plants are fresh (look for the week number on the wrapper). Buy from a greengrocer's only as a last resort, especially in winter. House plants come from warm countries and don't enjoy draughty December days on British pavements.

With Christmas pot plants you've no option but to buy in winter; other pot plants can be more safely transported home in spring and summer when temperatures are higher and they are growing more rapidly.

Whatever the time of year, insist that the plant is well wrapped up. Get it home as quickly as possible, and don't leave it to freeze or fry in the car.

What makes a good plant?

Biggest doesn't always mean best in the house plant world.

Look for a plant that has:
- A good shape
- No browning at the leaf tips
- No pests

Use dilute tomato fertiliser to get any flower-shy pot plant to produce blooms.

- Moist compost around the roots
- A perky appearance

Avoid plants that have:

- Wilting leaves
- Greenfly or other pests
- Disease-spotted leaves
- Dry and shrunken compost
- Bare stems
- Any kind of damage

If you're buying a flowering plant, choose one that has some blooms fully open and some in bud. Plants in full flower may fade quickly; those in tight bud may refuse to open when you get them home.

The choice

For goodness sake choose a plant that will enjoy living with you. Don't check its requirements *after* you've bought it; look at the following lists *before* you buy to find the right plant for the corner you want to fill.

For unheated rooms Adiantum (maidenhair fern), Araucaria (Norfolk Island pine), Aspidistra, Beloperone (shrimp plant), Billbergia (queen's tears), Browallia, Calceolaria (slipper flower), Campanula, Chlorophytum (spider plant), Chrysanthemum, Citrus (orange), Cordyline, Cyclamen, Cytisus (broom), Erica (Cape heath), Fatshedera, Fatsia (false castor oil palm), Hedera (ivy), Hydrangea, Pelargonium (geranium), Primula, Rhododendron (azalea), Rhoicissus (grape ivy), Saxifraga (mother-of-thousands), Senecio (cineraria), Soleirolia (mind-your-own-business, baby's tears).

For centrally-heated rooms Aechmea (urn plant), Aglaeonema, Anthurium (flamingo flower), Aphelandra (zebra plant), Begonia, Chlorophytum (spider plant), Codiaeum (croton, Joseph's coat), Columnea, Dieffenbachia (dumb cane), Dizygotheca (finger aralia), Dracaena (dragon tree), Epipremnum (devil's ivy, scindapsus), Euphorbia (poinsettia), Ficus (fig, rubber plant), Heptapleurum (umbrella tree), Howea (palm), Hoya (wax plant), Maranta (prayer plant), Monstera (Swiss cheese plant), Pandanus (screw pine), Peperomia (pepper plant), Philodendron (sweetheart plant), Pilea (aluminium plant),

Plectranthus, Rhoicissus (grape ivy), Saintpaulia (African violet), Sansevieria (mother-in-law's tongue), Schefflera, Sinningia (gloxinia), Stephanotis, Streptocarpus (Cape primrose), Yucca (ti tree).

For shady corners Adiantum (maidenhair fern), Asparagus, Aspidistra, Asplenium (bird's nest fern), Cissus (kangaroo vine), Fatshedera, Fatsia (false castor oil palm), Fittonia (net leaf), Maranta (prayer plant), Nephrolepis (ladder fern), Pellaea (button fern), Peperomia (pepper plant), Philodendron (sweetheart plant), Pilea (aluminium plant), Platycerium (stag's horn fern), Plectranthus, Rhoicissus (grape ivy), Sansevieria (mother-in-law's tongue), Soleirolia (mind-your-own-business, baby's tears).

For windowsills Browallia, Campanula, Capsicum (pepper), Coleus (flame nettle), Crassula, Cryptanthus (earth stars), Cyclamen, Dionaea (Venus' fly trap), Erica (Cape heath), Fuchsia, Hedera (ivy), Impatiens (busy lizzie), Kalanchoe, Nertera (bead plant), Pelargonium (geranium), Plectranthus, Primula, Rhododendron (azalea), Saintpaulia (African violet), Sansevieria (mother-in-law's tongue), Saxifraga (mother of thousands), Schlumbergera (Christmas cactus), Senecio (cineraria), Setcreasea, Solanum (Christmas pepper), Soleirolia (mind-your-own-business, baby's tears), Tradescantia (wandering sailor), Zebrina.

For warm bathrooms Adiantum (maidenhair fern), Aechmea (urn plant), Aglaeonema, Anthurium (flamingo flower), Aphelandra (zebra plant), Asparagus, Asplenium (bird's nest fern), Begonia, Beloperone (shrimp plant), Billbergia (queen's tears), Codiaeum (croton, Joseph's coat), Cryptanthus (earth stars), Cyperus (umbrella grass), Dieffenbachia (dumb cane), Dionaea (Venus' fly trap), Dracaena (dragon tree), Epipremnum (devil's ivy), Fittonia (net leaf), Maranta (prayer plant), Nephrolepis (ladder fern), Pellaea (button fern), Peperomia (pepper plant), Pilea (aluminium plant), Platycerium (stag's horn fern), Plectranthus, Pteris (ribbon fern), Saintpaulia (African violet), Tradescantia (wandering sailor), Zebrina.

Architectural specimen plants Araucaria (Norfolk

Ferns grow well in a warm bathroom see opposite for ideas

Island pine), Codiaeum (croton, Joseph's coat), Cordyline, Cycas (cycad), Dizygotheca (finger aralia), Dracaena (dragon tree), Fatsia (false castor oil palm), Ficus (fig, rubber plant), Heptapleurum (umbrella tree), Howea (palm), Monstera (Swiss cheese plant), Pandanus (screw pine), Philodendron (sweetheart plant), Sansevieria (mother-in-law's tongue), Schefflera, Yucca (ti tree).

When ferns become brown and tatty, snip off all the fronds 1in (2.5cm) above the compost and stand the plant on a gravel tray to encourage healthy growth.

Climbers for screens and tripods Cissus (kangaroo vine), Epipremnum (devil's ivy), Fatshedera, Hedera (ivy), *Hoya carnosa* (wax plant), Jasminum (white jasmine), Philodendron (sweetheart plant), Rhoicissus (grape ivy), Stephanotis.

Plants that are difficult to kill Asparagus, Beloperone (shrimp plant), Chlorophytum (spider plant), Cissus (kangaroo vine), Cyperus (umbrella grass), Heptapleurum (umbrella tree), Philodendron (sweetheart plant), Plectranthus, Rhoicissus, Sansevieria (mother-in-law's tongue) – except by overwatering, Tradescantia.

PLANTS AT HOME

Once you've lugged your chosen plant home its battle for survival begins. It *wants* to live, so all you have to do is provide it with reasonable growing conditions.

Unpack the plant as soon as possible and stand it in good light but not brilliant sunshine. Even plants that like full light will appreciate a day's breather to get used to the atmosphere of their new home. If the compost in the pot is dry, soak it thoroughly with tepid water.

After a day or two, put the plant in its permanent spot. If it's being positioned on its own, a pot-hider or saucer will smarten up the container and prevent any drips from marking your Chippendale furniture. Plants grouped together are happiest when stood on a tray of moist gravel which keeps the air around them pleasantly humid.

Keep all house plants out of these deathtraps:
- Near radiators
- In draughts or behind closed curtains at night
- Places where they are constantly knocked.

How much light?

All plants need light, but some can put up with less than others, and these are the ones to choose for your shady corners (see list on page 14).

Most plants enjoy what the experts call 'good, indirect light', which is the kind found 1 to 2m (3 to 6ft) from a window. Some, like pelargoniums (geraniums, to you)

Fatshedera will grow in an unheated room or shady corner

and impatients (busy lizzies) adore full sunlight and will not flower freely in anything else. Plants that become spindly and 'drawn' are almost certainly not getting enough light – even shade lovers need a certain amount of brightness. Hold the book at arm's length in the spot chosen for the plant and try to read this small print:

If you find it impossible to read this, then one of two things is likely; either there is insufficient light to grow shade-loving plants; or you need a new pair of glasses. Or both.

How much heat?

Most plants prefer to be warm during the day and cool at night; the state of affairs in most homes. But some plants don't enjoy high temperatures at any time and are guaranteed to suffer if kept too warm:

- Cyclamen
- Erica (Cape heath)
- Rhododendron (azalea)
- Senecio (cineraria)

This little lot will grow well only in cool rooms where the temperature hovers around the 13 to 16°C mark (55 to 60°F). That's too cold for most warm-blooded central-heating lovers, so keep these plants in cool halls or bedrooms.

Use the lists on pages 13 and 14 as a guide to find plants that will cope with your heating, or lack of it.

Humidity

Brown-edged leaves are a common sight on lots of house plants and the cause is almost always dry air. There isn't one plant that won't benefit from extra humidity in the home and it's as easy as pie to provide. Simply stand the plant or group of plants on a tray of gravel which can be kept moist at all times. Alternatively fill a deeper dish with moist peat and plunge the pots into it.

Single specimen plants can be sprayed over daily with tepid rainwater from a hand mister, but watch your furniture!

Watering

Ninety-nine per cent of all house plant deaths are caused by overwatering. So be careful! A house plant will quickly recover from wilt due to underwatering; it will seldom recover from wilt due to overwatering.
Question: How often do I water it?
Answer: When it's dry.

Choose an azalea for winter colour in an unheated room

Look at the compost in the pot, then feel it with your fingers. If it's dusty on the surface it's probably dry right the way through. If it feels like a freshly wrung-out flannel then it's still moist.

If you can't see or feel the compost because of the tightly packed foliage, get used to weighing the plant in your hand. When dry it will feel very light.

Peaty composts shrink when they are dry. Watch for a fine crack between the edge of the compost and the pot — don't wait until it turns into a chasm.

When a plant *is* dry, soak it thoroughly from the top, unless you can't fit the spout of your watering can or jug among the rosette of leaves. If this is the case (it's very likely with African violets and cyclamens), stand the plant in a bowl of water for half an hour, then remove it. During that time it will have taken up all the water it needs. Don't water again until the compost is dry once more.

There are four exceptions to the watering rule:
● Bromeliads (pineapple family)
● Cyperus (umbrella grass)
● Ferns
● Rhododendrons (azaleas)

Grow a few half-hardy annuals as temporary pot plants on a sunny windowsill.

Ferns should be kept slightly moist at all times; rhododendrons and cyperus should be kept very moist. Bromeliads with 'vases' of leaves should always have some water in their vase.

Test your plants for water daily in summer; weekly in winter – they'll require much less water between October and March.

Hydroculture

The coward's way out! A hydroculture unit is a reservoir of water over which is suspended a plastic basket of expanded clay granules through which the plant's roots grow. Each unit looks like a plastic box and has a small indicator on the side which shows when the water in the reservoir needs topping up. The plant absorbs all the water it needs, and special liquid fertiliser can be diluted in the water.

The units are bought ready planted and are very easy to manage. Don't confuse them with self-watering pots which contain compost and a series of wicks leading to a

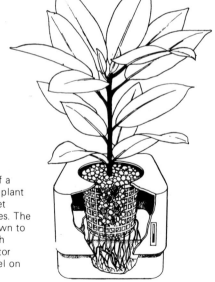

A cut-away diagram of a hydroculture unit. The plant is supported in a basket containing clay granules. The feeding roots grow down to absorb the nutrient-rich water. Note the indicator showing the water level on the right

reservoir below. I've yet to see a plant growing really well in one of these units, while those in the hydroculture pots seem to thrive.

Feeding

Plants need food as well as drink, but they can only absorb it in liquid form. Diluted liquid feeds can be watered on to the moist compost in the pot once a month

A bromeliad such as *Neoregelia carolinae* 'Tricolor' always needs some water in its 'vase'

Never be afraid to replace tired pot plants by taking a few cuttings from them and ditching the aged relative.

from March to October. Only Christmas- and winter-flowering pot plants need be fed between November and February.

Idlers can sprinkle slow-release plant-food granules on to the surface of the compost at any time. These will take a small amount of food to the roots every time the plant is watered.

Pot plant fertiliser is widely available, but all flowering house plants enjoy liquid tomato fertiliser which promotes blooming. Use it at the dilution rate recommended for tomatoes, except on very young plants which will prefer half strength. It works a treat in coaxing flower-shy African violets into bloom.

Foliar feeds can be used on all plants except ferns and those which have hairy leaves. The diluted solution is sprayed on to the foliage, which should be kept out of full sunshine until the spray has dried off.

Newly potted plants will not need feeding for a couple of months.

Pots and compost

Sooner or later the plant you buy is going to need a larger pot and more compost. You can see how it's getting along by carefully turning it upside down and tapping off its pot against a hard surface. If roots can be seen wrapped around the outside of the compost, the plant is 'pot bound'. One or two house plants prefer to be in this state for quite some time – African violets flower well if pot bound and the mother-in-law's tongue (sansevieria) should not be potted on until it cracks its existing pot – but others will enjoy a move to more spacious accommodation once a year.

Spring and summer are the times to 'pot on' your plants. Choose a plastic pot that is 5cm (2in) larger in diameter than the existing one.

There are two basic kinds of compost suitable for pot plants: the soilless type based on peat, and the John Innes composts.

Peat-based composts are:
- Light
- Clean

Arrange small pot plants in groups in large bowls of gravel or peat – they'll enjoy the company.

(a) Knock the plant out of its old pot
(b) Set it in the new pot on a bed of compost
(c) Add compost around the root ball, firming as you go

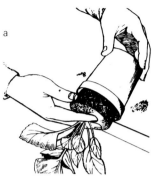

- Easy to use
- Difficult to re-wet if allowed to dry out
- Lacking in nutrients after six weeks
- Likely to shrink when dry

John Innes composts are:

- Heavy enough to support top-heavy plants
- Easy to moisten when dry
- Retentive of nutrients
- Variable in quality

Newly rooted house plants can be potted in John Innes No.1 potting compost; the majority of house plants in No.2 compost, and the really vigorous types in No.3 compost which contains most fertiliser. Peat-based compost are suitable for a wide range of plants.

Water the plant thoroughly the day before repotting it. When you're ready to pot, this is what to do:

1. Spread a layer of compost in the base of the pot
2. Knock the plant from its pot and sit it in the new one
3. Feed in compost around the rootball
4. Firm it with your fingers (lightly if it's peat-based)
5. Add more compost until the pot is full
6. When the job is finished the surface of the compost should be 1 to 2cm ($\frac{1}{2}$ to 1in) below the rim of the pot
7. Water the plant by standing it in a bowl of water until the surface of the compost is evenly moist.

Plants in very large pots can be topdressed each spring instead of being potted on. Scrape away 5 to 8cm (2 to 3in) of compost on the surface and replace it with fresh.

Cleaning up

Just like the rest of your furniture, house plants get dusty. They need light if they are to thrive, and a layer of grime prevents the sun from reaching the leaf surfaces. Flick a feather duster over them if you like, but they'll be more effectively cleaned with a tissue or piece of kitchen roll dipped in rainwater or a mixture of equal parts of water and milk (which seems to give them added lustre).

The new 'leaf-shine wipes' which can be bought in small drums with a flip-top are very efficient, but it's a good idea to test both these and aerosol leaf cleaners on a

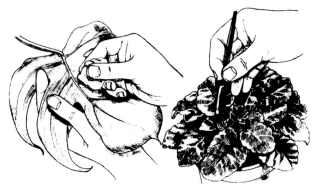

Clean the leaves of your house plants regularly

Grow small bromeliads on an old tree branch planted in a pot. Wrap their roots in sphagnum moss and wire them to the stems.

single leaf before treating the entire plant. Never use leaf-cleaning chemicals on:

- Hairy-leaved plants
- Ferns

Ferns are happy being washed clean with a spray of rainwater; hairy-leaved plants such as African violets should be brushed free of dust with a clean paintbrush.

Stephanotis needs holding up!

Holding up

Single-stemmed plants can be supported with a single cane and loops of soft twine. Bushy plants can be held up either with small twiggy branches pushed among the foliage, or by a trio of split green canes encircled with twine to form an enclosure. If the plants seem tough enough to support themselves, let them do so.

Plants such as monstera and philodendron are often supported by moss-covered sticks. These are the very devil to keep moist and will usually shed their moss on to your carpet. Replace them with stout canes if necessary, and lead any aerial roots into the compost within the pot.

Climbing plants can have their stems trained up tripods of canes, or over pieces of trelliswork fastened to walls. Stephanotis is often trained around a hoop of wire so that its flowers are shown off well, but it will be equally happy on a tripod.

Shaping up

Some house plants need a bit of pruning to keep them shapely and within bounds. Bushy plants that have a tendency to become lanky or 'leggy' should have their shoot tips pinched out regularly (but bear in mind that you may lose flower buds if you do the job too frequently). Vine-like climbers such as:

- Cissus
- Hedera (ivy)
- Philodendron
- Rhoicissus

can be thinned from time to time and whole stems removed. Do the job in spring for preference; at any time of year if you're desperate.

Large plants with one or two stems that look like taking over the house can be mercilessly hacked back in spring. Cut them back to just above a healthy leaf and new shoots will soon sprout. This treatment is suitable for:

- Fatsia
- Ficus (rubber plant)
- Heptapleurum
- Monstera
- Schefflera

Bushy plants that are tired or brown can sometimes be chopped off right at compost level in spring, repotted and allowed to grow again. Try the trick with:

- Adiantum
- Asparagus
- Beloperone
- Campanula
- Coleus
- Impatiens
- Nephrolepis
- Pelargonium
- Plectranthus
- Primula

On holiday

The most reliable form of holiday care for house plants comes in the form of a green-fingered neighbour who can be left with instructions. Failing this good fortune you'll have to make alternative arrangements.

Plants watered well and plunged in plastic seed trays filled with moist peat will often go for two weeks without water if they are kept in a cool room that receives no direct sunlight.

Alternatively you can try capillary watering. This flashy term is used to describe the passage of water from a piece of nylon matting up through the compost in the pot. Here's what to do:

1. Place a washing-up bowl in the sink and fill it with water.
2. Lead a piece of capillary matting (sold by garden centres) from the bowl up on to the draining board.
3. Stand the plants on the matting.
4. Check that it is moist before you leave.

Hey presto! The plants should drink what they want while you're away.

Remember that this scheme only works with plants in plastic pots. Plants in clay pots should be provided with wicks – short lengths of the matting material – to bridge the gap between the base of the compost and the mat.

This capillary watering system is a good way of ensuring your plants don't dry out while you are away

Grow your own pineapple plant by rotting a pineapple top in peat and sand. You'll have to wait a while for fruits though!

Try brightening up your kitchen with a few house plants; *Ficus pumila*, the creeping fig will enjoy the warmth

A to Z of House Plants

Somewhere here are the plants that will be happiest growing in your home. I've not stuck to the thermometer when recommending suitable temperatures for the plants. You know yourself which of your rooms are warm (usually the sitting room and often the bathroom), which are cool (usually the bedrooms) and which are unheated (guest rooms when the guest has flown). Plonk the plant where you think it will do best, bearing in mind the information given.

Adiantum (Maidenhair fern)

Feathery bright green fronds on black fuse-wire stems. **Height**: 30cm (1ft). **Spread**: 45cm (1½ft). **Temperature**: Cool room. **Light**: Indirect light or gentle shade. Not full sun. **Cultivation**: Keep the compost constantly moist and feed monthly in summer. Place on a tray of moist gravel to improve humidity. Badly browned specimens should be cut down to within 2.5cm (1in) of compost and stood on a gravel tray to revive them. Will crisp up in full sun or near radiators. Do not use insecticides or leaf cleaners. Low temperatures, moist compost and a humid atmosphere are the keys to success. Propagate by dividing mature clumps in spring.

Aechmea (Urn plant)

A large, leathery 'vase' of leaves often centred with a spiky pink flower cluster. **Height**: 45cm (1½ft). **Spread**: 45cm (1½ft). **Temperature**: Warm room. **Light**: Good indirect light, not bright sun or deep shade. **Cultivation**: Keep the 'vase' topped up with water at all times. Monthly foliar feeds will be enjoyed in summer. Stand on a gravel tray for ample humidity. Central rosette dies as flower fades; side shoots take over and can be potted up.

Aphelandra (Zebra plant)

Cream-veined leaves and cockades of bright yellow flowers in summer. **Height and spread**: 30cm (1ft). **Temperature**: Warm room. **Light**: Good indirect light.

Aechmea produces a
splendid pink flower spike
(See page 29)

Cultivation: Keep moist (not soggy) at all times and feed
monthly in summer. Stand on a gravel tray to increase
humidity. Cut back straggly plants in spring. Propagate
by shoot tip cuttings in summer. Shade, low temperatures
or dry air may cause leaf drop.

Asparagus (Asparagus fern)

Frothy and feathery-leaved plants with bright green
foliage on arching or upright stems. **Height:** 30cm (1ft).
Spread: 60cm (2ft). **Temperature:** Cool or warm room;
very adaptable. **Light:** Indirect light or gentle shade.
Cultivation: Water when compost feels dry on the
surface. Feed fortnightly in summer. Enjoys a gravel tray.
Congested plants can be divided in spring. Snip off
yellowing fronds. Dry air causes leaf fall.

Aspidistra (Cast iron plant)

Bold, arching leaves of rich deep green. **Height and
spread:** 60cm (2ft). **Temperature:** Cool or unheated
room. **Light:** Indirect light or shade. **Cultivation:** Allow
compost to dry out between waterings. Feed monthly in
summer. Repot only when pot bound and there is no room
for more leaves to develop. Propagate by division in
spring. Overwatering is the biggest cause of failure.

Asplenium (Bird's nest fern)

A bright green shuttlecock of broad leaves. **Height and
spread:** 60cm (2ft). **Temperature:** Warm room. **Light:**

Plants that produce aerial roots do so because they need
them – don't chop them off; instead lead them towards the
compost or a moss-covered stick.

Gentle shade or indirect light. **Cultivation**: Keep compost gently moist at all times and feed monthly in summer. Stand on a gravel tray. Snip off brown fronds (caused by dry air, draughts or sun scorch). Don't use leaf-shine products. Propagation is difficult without spoiling the plant.

Begonia

A diverse group of plants grown for both leaf and flower beauty with similar cultivation requirements. **Height**: From 15cm (6in) to 1m (3ft) with varying spreads. **Temperature**: Warm room. **Light**: Good indirect light. **Cultivation**: Water when compost feels dry. Feed fortnightly in summer. Allow tuberous begonias to dry out completely in winter, storing the tubers in a cool, dry place. Start them into growth in fresh compost in spring. Stand on a gravel tray in summer. Divide clump formers in spring; take leaf cuttings of *B. rex*; sow seeds of *B.*

Begonia rex can easily be propagated from leaf cuttings

It is easy to see why beloperone is known as the shrimp plant

semperflorens. Flower drop is usually caused by dryness of atmosphere or dryness at the roots. Cut back straggly plants in spring; shoot tips can be used as cuttings.

Beloperone (Shrimp plant)

Downy green leaves topped with arching pink bracts. **Height and spread:** 60cm (2ft). **Temperature:** Warm or cool room. **Light:** Good light, or bright sun. **Cultivation:** Keep compost gently moist at all times; feed fortnightly in summer. Stand on a gravel tray. Cut back to 8cm (3in) and repot each spring. Divide or take cuttings in spring.

Capsicum (Christmas pepper)

Pointed red, orange, yellow and purple berries in winter. **Height:** 30cm (1ft). **Spread:** 15cm (6in). **Temperature:** Cool room. **Light:** Full sun. **Cultivation:** Keep compost gently moist at all times; feed fortnightly in summer. Spray open flowers with water. Propagate by seeds sown in spring. Discard when fruits shrivel.

Chamaedorea (Parlour palm)

Miniature palm tree. **Height:** Up to 1m (3ft). **Spread:** 45cm (1½ft). **Temperature:** Cool or warm room. **Light:**

'Fresh air plants' are bromeliads that can live without compost. Simply spray them with rainwater or distilled water daily.

Good, indirect. **Cultivation**: Keep compost gently moist; feed monthly in summer. Stand on gravel tray. Propagate by seeds sown in spring. Bright sun or dry air causes leaf scorch.

Chlorophytum (Spider plant)

Fountains of variegated leaves and plantlets on long wands. **Height**: 45cm (1½ft). **Spread**: 60cm (2ft). **Temperature**: Warm or cool room. **Light**: Good but indirect light. **Cultivation**: Keep compost gently moist at all times; feed fortnightly in summer. Lack of water and/or

The popular spider plant, chlorophytum, is very easy going

Codiaeums with their exotic and multicoloured foliage need warmth and moisture to succeed

nutrients causes leaf tips to turn brown. Pot on annually. Propagate by potting up plantlets.

Chrysanthemum

Dwarfed for one season, available in a wide range of colours at any time of year. **Height**: 23cm (9in). **Spread**: 30cm (1ft). **Temperature**: Cool room. **Light**: Bright light. **Cultivation**: Water when compost feels dry; feed fortnightly when in flower. Buy a plant with one or two buds already open. Discard when flowers fade.

Cissus (Kangaroo vine)

Bright green leaves with scalloped edges on a vine-like plant. **Height**: 1m+ (3ft+). **Spread**: 60cm+(2ft+).

Go over your plants regularly with a sharp knife to cut off faded leaves and the tips out of spindly shoots to encourage a bushy habit.

Temperature: Cool room. **Light**: Indirect or gentle shade. **Cultivation**: Water when compost feels dry; feed fortnightly in summer. Spray occasionally with water. Train over supports. Prune back unwanted stems in spring and take cuttings at the same time.

Citrus (Orange; lemon)

Bright green leaves, white scented flowers and, hopefully, some fruits. **Height and spread**: 1m (3ft) or so. **Temperature**: Cool room. **Light**: Bright. **Cultivation**: Water when compost feels dry; feed fortnightly and stand outdoors in summer. Spray with water occasionally. Prune in spring if necessary and use shoot tips as cuttings.

Codiaeum (Croton; Joseph's coat)

Leathery, multicoloured leaves, often with indented edges. **Height**: 1m + (3ft +). **Spread**: 45cm (1½ft). **Temperature**: Warm room. **Light**: Good, indirect. **Cultivation**: Keep gently moist at all times and feed monthly in summer. Stand on a gravel tray for maximum humidity. Lower leaves fall if plants are too dry, hungry, cold or in draughts. Generosity is the key to success. Cuttings can be taken in spring and summer. Snip back straggly shoots in spring.

Coleus (Flame nettle)

Nettle-like plants (no stings attached!) with vividly painted leaves and blue flower spires (which are best removed to encourage leaf production). **Height and spread**: 60cm (2ft). **Temperature**: Warm room. **Light**: Full sun. **Cultivation**: Water when compost feels dry; feed fortnightly in summer. Pinch out shoot tips regularly to encourage bushiness. Can become tatty in winter, in which case cut hard back in spring and pot on. Propagate by shoot tip cuttings in spring and summer; by seeds sown in spring. Discard after a couple of years.

Crassula (Money tree; jade plant)

Branching succulent with rounded, fleshy green leaves. **Height and spread**: 30cm + (1ft +). **Temperature**: Cool room. **Light**: Full sun. **Cultivation**: Water when surface

To obtain the best foliage effect it is good policy to pinch out the flower spikes of coleus as they appear

of compost feels dusty. Keep very much on dry side in winter. Feed monthly in summer. Propagate from stem cuttings in summer.

Cryptanthus (Earth stars)

Star-shaped rosettes of spiny, stripey leaves. **Height:** 5–15cm (2–6in). **Spread:** 10–23cm (4–9in). **Temperature:** Warm room. **Light:** Full sun. **Cultivation:** Keep gently moist at all times; use foliar feed two or three times during the summer. Stand on a gravel tray or spray daily with water. Best grown potbound or on 'trees' (wrap the plants' roots in sphagnum moss and strap them to an old wooden branch 'planted' in a flower pot). Water by daily misting.

Cyclamen (Sowbread)

Rounded, marbled leaves and bright flowers. **Height and spread:** 30cm (1ft). **Temperature:** Cool room (*very* important). **Light:** Bright, but not direct sun; north-facing window ideal. **Cultivation:** Water only when the surface of the compost is dry to the touch and from below when

Clay pots 'ring' when tapped if the compost is dry. Make a small wooden mallet as a water-requirement indicator; moist compost turns the 'ring' into a dull thud.

the leaf canopy is dense. Feed fortnightly when in flower. Stand on gravel tray. Repot every summer and pinch off flowers in summer to save energy for winter. Plant flops if overwatered or too warm.

Cyperus (Umbrella grass; papyrus)

Tall, pithy stems topped with umbrella-spoke leaves. **Height:** 30cm to 1.5m (1 to 5ft). **Spread:** 60cm (2ft). **Temperature:** Cool or warm room. **Light:** Indirect or gentle shade. **Cultivation:** Stand pot in a bowl of water to keep constantly moist. Feed monthly in summer. Cut off stalks as leaves fade. Divide mature plants in spring to propagate.

Dieffenbachia (Dumb cane)

Large oval leaves of green marbled with white. **Height:** 60cm–1.5m (2–5ft). **Spread:** 45cm (1½ft). **Temperature:** Warm room. **Light:** Good, indirect. **Cultivation:** Keep compost gently moist at all times; feed monthly in

Cyclamen are lovely house plants but so often fail. They need a cool bright room to be at their best

Dieffenbachia, dumb cane, has spectacular foilage but beware, the sap is poisonous

summer. Stand on a gravel tray. Pull off faded leaves. Propagate by removing offsets in spring. The sap is poisonous so keep out of the reach of children.

Dizygotheca (Finger aralia)

Dark brown hand-shaped leaves with saw-edges. **Height:** 2m (6ft). **Spread:** 60cm + (2ft +). **Temperature:** Warm room. **Light:** Indirect or gentle shade. **Cultivation:** Gently moist compost; feed monthly in summer. Stand on gravel tray. Cut back tall and lanky specimens in spring. Leaf drop is caused by dry air, dry or wet compost, or draughts. Propagate by seeds sown in spring.

Dracaena (Dragon tree)

Huge fountains of broad or narrow, often brightly striped leaves on a stout stem. **Height:** 1m+ (3ft+). **Spread:** 45cm+ (1½ft+). **Temperature:** Warm room. **Light:** Good, indirect. **Cultivation:** Water when surface of compost feels dry to the touch; feed fortnightly in summer. Stand on a gravel tray or mist daily. Remove flower stems – they spoil the plant's shape. Propagate by sowing seeds in spring or from root cuttings. Peel off faded leaves. Cut-back stumps will usually sprout again. Air layer to reduce a plant's height.

Epipremnum (Devil's ivy; scindapsus)

Heart-shaped variegated leaves on a scrambling vine of a plant. **Height:** Incalculable. **Temperature:** Warm room. **Light:** Good but indirect. **Cultivation:** Water when surface of compost feels dry; feed monthly in summer. Spray daily with water. Pull off faded leaves regularly; train over a support system. Propagate by cuttings in summer. Pinch out shoot tips to encourage bushiness.

Euphorbia (Poinsettia)

Bright red, pink or white bracts surround the tiny flowers in winter; handsome green leaves. **Height and spread:** Usually dwarfed to about 30cm (1ft) but up to 1m (3ft) both ways if not dwarfed by nurseryman. **Temperature:** Warm room. **Light:** Good, indirect. **Cultivation:** Water when compost feels dry on the surface. Feed fortnightly in summer. Mist with water occasionally. When bracts fade cut plant back to 10cm (4in). To encourage bracts to redden, keep the plant in a darkened place each night from 6pm until 8am for two months before flowers are desired. Plants which do not get such 'long nights' will stay green. Repot every spring.

Fatshedera (Fat-headed lizzie; ivy tree)

Glossy green, hand-shaped leaves on clambering stems. **Height:** Considerable if trained up a support. **Temperature:** Cool room. **Light:** Indirect or gentle shade. **Cultivation:** Water when compost feels dry; feed

Turn an old tropical fish tank into a home for miniature ferns – they'll enjoy the humidity.

Poinsettia is a favourite plant at Christmas

monthly in summer. Spray occasionally with water. Provide support system if plant is to climb, otherwise it will trail. Pinch to encourage bushiness. Propagate by summer cuttings.

Fatsia (Fig-leaf palm; false castor oil palm)

Large glossy, hand-shaped leaves, usually on a single-stemmed plant. **Height and spread:** 1m+ (3ft+). **Temperature:** Cool room. **Light:** Indirect or gentle shade. **Cultivation:** Water when compost feels dry; feed monthly in summer. Spray occasionally with water. Keep leaves clean. Propagate by removal of offsets in summer; by seeds in spring. Hardy outside when too big for the house.

Ficus (Fig; rubber plant)

A varied group of foliage plants with plain green or variegated leaves and statuesque habits. **Height:** Vary

Ficus elastica   *Ficus benjamina*

between ground hugging (creeping fig) and several metres. **Temperature**: Warm or cool rooms. **Light**: Good indirect for taller kinds; gentle shade for creeping fig. **Cultivation**: Water when the surface of the compost feels dry. Feed monthly in summer. Stand on a gravel tray. Stake if necessary. Air layer overtall rubber plants in spring. Take cuttings in summer.

Fittonia (Snakeskin plant; net leaf)

Green leaves with creamy white or pink veins. **Height**: 2.5–15cm (1in–6in). **Spread**: 30cm (1ft). **Temperature**: Warm room. **Light**: Indirect or gentle shade. **Cultivation**: Keep gently moist; slightly drier in winter. Feed monthly in summer. Stand on gravel tray (it hates dry air). Propagate by division in spring. Pinching back the shoots encourages bushiness.

Hedera (Ivy)

Plain green leaved, finely cut or variegated varieties. **Height**: Endless, can cascade. **Temperature**: Cool room; no heat needed. **Light**: Good indirect for variegated

African violets will flower more willingly in winter with additional lighting from a fluorescent tube suspended 1ft (30cm) or so above them.

types; green varieties can take gentle shade. **Cultivation**: Water when surface of compost feels dry. Feed monthly in summer. Spray daily with water. Pinch out shoot tips to encourage a fuller habit. Cuttings root readily in spring and summer.

Hippeastrum (Amaryllis)

Trumpet flowers at the top of stout stalks in winter; strappy leaves come later. **Height**: 60cm (2ft). **Spread**: 45cm (1½ft). **Temperature**: Warm room. **Light**: Good, indirect. **Cultivation**: Pot up bulb in early winter in moist compost and water *very* sparingly until flower opens. Feed fortnightly during summer. Water more generously as foliage appears, stop in midsummer and dry off bulb. Chop off leaves and place bulb in airing cupboard for a week before storing in a cool place. Knock out of old compost and repot in fresh in early winter.

Busy lizzie can easily be grown from cuttings and is available in a range of flower and foliage colours

Howea (Kentia palm)

Handsome palms with arching fronds – denizens of the palm court. **Height and spread:** 2m (6ft). **Temperature:** Warm room. **Light:** Indirect or gentle shade. **Cultivation:** Keep compost gently moist (not soggy). Feed monthly in summer. Spray daily with water or stand on gravel tray. Snip off brown fronds. Dry air, draughts or scorching sun cause browning. Propagate by sowing seeds in spring.

Impatiens (Busy lizzie)

Fleshy stems, green or purple leaves and bright, round flowers during much of the year. **Height and spread:** Up to 60cm (2ft). **Temperature:** Warm room. **Light:** Bright but not scorching sun. **Cultivation:** Keep gently moist at all times and feed fortnightly in summer. Cut back and pot on each spring. Propagate from cuttings in spring and summer or by sowing seeds. Pinch out shoot tips to encourage bushiness.

Maranta (Prayer plant; herringbone plant)

Oval leaves marked with brown and sometimes pink in herringbone fashion. **Height:** 15cm (6in). **Spread:** 30cm (1ft). **Temperature:** Warm room. **Light:** Gentle shade. **Cultivation:** Keep evenly moist at all times; feed monthly in summer. Stand on gravel tray; hates dry air. Wet compost and cold are likely causes of failure. Propagate by cuttings or division in spring.

Monstera (Swiss cheese plant)

Huge heart-shaped leaves full of holes (when mature). **Height:** To your ceiling. **Spread:** 2m (6ft) or so. **Temperature:** Warm room. **Light:** Indirect or gentle shade. **Cultivation:** Water when compost feels dry; feed monthly in summer. Spray daily with water. Stake to keep upright. Cut back hard when overgrown – it will sprout again. Lead aerial roots into pot – don't cut them off. Pull off faded leaves. Clean leaves regularly. Propagate by cuttings in summer.

Many house plants are happy outdoors between June and September, but make sure they're not scorched by bright sun – dappled sunlight suits them best.

This Victorian Wardian case provides the ideal environment for ferns to thrive indoors

Nephrolepis (Ladder fern)

Arching fronds of bright green that make huge fountains.
Height and spread: 60cm (2ft). **Temperature:** Warm room. **Light:** Indirect or gentle shade. **Cultivation:** Keep gently moist at all times and feed monthly in summer. Loathes dry air so stand on a gravel tray or mist daily. Difficult to grow in hanging baskets without browning. Propagate by division in spring when tatty plants can be cut back hard and grown again in a more moist atmosphere.

Make a bottle garden from an old cider flagon, carboy or sweet jar. Small and slow-growing plants will enjoy its sheltered confines.

Philodendron (Sweetheart plant)

Climbers or bushy plants, often with heart-shaped leaves. Most are very vigorous. **Height and spread:** Up to 2m (6ft) or more. **Temperature:** Warm room. **Light:** Indirect or gentle shade. **Cultivation:** Water when compost feels dry; feed monthly in summer. Most need support. Cut back shoots to encourage bushiness. Stand on gravel tray or spray daily with water. Propagate by shoot-tip cuttings in spring and summer.

Pilea (Aluminium plant)

Small plant with glossy green leaves spotted with grey. **Height and spread:** 23cm (9in). **Temperature:** Warm room. **Light:** Indirect. **Cultivation:** Water when compost feels dry; feed monthly in summer. Stand on gravel tray. Pinch out shoot tips to encourage bushiness. Take stem cuttings in summer.

Platycerium (Stag's horn fern)

Fronds shaped like antlers and covered in down. **Height and spread:** 45cm (1½ft). **Temperature:** Warm room. **Light:** Gentle shade. **Cultivation:** Keep gently moist at all times; feed monthly in summer. Stand on gravel tray or strap to a log and spray daily with rainwater. Dunk log-grown plants in a bucket of water when compost or moss around roots is dry. Never clean fronds.

Primula

Dainty flowering plants that may be had in bloom at most times of year. **Height and spread:** 15–30cm (6in–1ft). **Temperature:** Cool room. **Light:** Sunny windowsill. **Cultivation:** Water when the compost feels dry; feed fortnightly when in flower. Stand on gravel tray. Propagate by sowing seeds in spring. Discard after flowering; polyanthuses can be planted outside.

Rhododendron (Azalea)

Mounds of evergreen leaves topped with rosettes of bloom in winter. **Height and spread:** 30cm (1ft).

Temperature: Cool room; no heat needed. **Light**: Bright, but not scorching sun. **Cultivation**: Keep compost moist at all times (water daily with rainwater). Feed fortnightly in summer. Stand on gravel tray. Plunge plant outdoors in the garden in summer; bring in before the frosts. Take cuttings in summer. Goes brown (or buds fail to open) if kept too hot or allowed to dry out at the roots.

Rhoicissus (Grape ivy)

Scrambling vine with deep green scalloped leaves, smaller than those of cissus and divided into threes. **Height and spread:** Considerable. **Temperature:** Warm or cool room. **Light:** Good or heavy shade (very tough). **Cultivation:** Water when compost feels dry; feed fortnightly in summer. Spray with water from time to time. Cut out straggly shoots and chop back hard in spring to rejuvenate straggly plants. Needs support. Propagate by taking shoot tip cuttings in summer.

Saintpaulia (African violet)

Small domes of downy leaves and bright clusters of flowers at any time of year. **Height:** 10cm (4in). **Spread:** Up to 30cm (1ft). **Temperature:** Warm room. **Light:** Bright but not scorching sun. **Cultivation:** Water when compost feels dry (get used to weighing the pot in your hand if leaves cover the compost). Water from below by standing in a bowl of water for half an hour. Feed every ten days with dilute tomato fertiliser to encourage blooming. Do not give too large a pot or plants will be shy of blooming. Stand on gravel tray. Propagate by leaf cuttings in spring and summer. Clean leaves with a dry brush. Repot every other spring. Remove faded leaves and flowers as soon as seen.

Sansevieria (Mother-in-law's tongue)

Sword-shaped leaves, mottled with grey or banded with creamy yellow. **Height:** Up to 1m (3ft). **Spread:** 30cm (1ft). **Temperature:** Warm or cool room. **Light:** Sun or shade. **Cultivation:** Water only when compost feels dry; feed monthly in summer. Best when pot bound. Divide mature clumps in spring. Keep dryish in winter.

Grow your own peanut plant from a nut (not a salted one!). Once the plant has flowered the blooms are pushed down under the surface of the compost where the nuts are formed.

Saintpaulia, the African violet, is another subject that can be raised from leaf cuttings

Schefflera (Umbrella tree; heptapleurum)

Green or variegated fingered leaves. **Height**: 2m+ (6ft+). **Spread**: 1m+ (3ft+). **Temperature**: Warm room. **Light**: Good indirect. **Cultivation**: Water when compost feels dry; feed monthly in summer. Spray daily with water. A good sized pot will help plants to retain their lower leaves. Propagate by seeds sown in spring.

Schlumbergera (Christmas cactus)

Flattened pads in arching formation shoot out cerise flowers in winter. New varieties have different-coloured blooms. **Height**: 30cm (1ft). **Spread**: 45cm (1½ft). **Temperature**: Cool room. **Light**: Good, indirect. **Cultivation**: Performs well in a hanging basket. Water when compost feels dry. Feed with tomato fertiliser once a month in summer. Spray daily in summer with water and stand or hang plant outdoors in dappled shade. Take cuttings in summer. Do not move plants once buds have been formed or they may drop.

Senecio (Cineraria)

Domes of green leaves topped with clusters of daisy flowers in shades of mauve and cerise. **Height and spread:** 30cm (1ft). **Temperature:** Very cool room. **Light:** Bright but not direct sun. **Cultivation:** Water only when dry (and plant just starts to wilt). Overwatering kills. Feed fortnightly when in flower. Stand on gravel tray. Propagate by seeds sown in early summer. Discard after flowering.

Solanum (Winter cherry)

Pale green leaves on busy plants that are laden with round orange berries in winter. **Height and spread:** 30cm (1ft). **Temperature:** Cool room; no heat needed. **Light:** Sunny

Christmas cactus looks attractive in a hanging basket

windowsill. **Cultivation**: Keep compost gently moist; feed monthly in summer, alternating ordinary feed with a solution of 1 teaspoonful of Epsom salts in a pint of water to prevent leaf yellowing. Spray open flowers with water to encourage fruit set. Sow seeds in spring and take cuttings during spring and summer. Cut back and pot up plants in spring, though they are best replaced. Plants are happy outdoors in summer.

Stephanotis (Madagascar jasmine; clustered wax flower)

Twining stems clothed with oval, glossy leaves and decorated with white, waxy, scented flowers between spring and autumn. **Height**: Dependant upon support system. **Temperature**: Warm room. **Light**: Good, indirect. **Cultivation**: Water when compost feels dry; feed fortnightly in summer. Spray daily with tepid water. Thin out shoots after flowering. Do not move plants in bloom or flowers may drop. Keep out of draughts. Cuttings of shoot tips can be taken in summer.

Tradescantia (Wandering Jew; wandering sailor)

Trailing plants that are difficult to kill. **Length**: 60cm (2ft) or so. **Temperature**: Cool room. **Light**: Full sun if possible. **Cultivation**: It will grow in spite of you rather than because of you. Water when compost feels dry; feed monthly in summer. Leaves turn brown in very hot or dry rooms. Daily spraying with water helps. Chop back straggly plants in spring. Cuttings root at any time.

Yucca (Spanish bayonet; ti tree)

Thick trunks that carry fountains of pointed green leaves. **Height**: Up to several metres. **Spread**: Not much. **Temperature**: Warm or cool room. **Light**: Bright spot. **Cultivation**: Water when compost feels dry; feed fortnightly in summer. Spray daily with water. Peel off faded leaves. Stand outdoors in summer. Propagate by cutting off 10-cm (4-in) lengths of stem and pushing them into moist compost; leaves will emerge. Overwatering can kill yuccas.

Cacti are ideal house plants for unheated rooms where they can be stood on bright windowsills. Cool winter temperatures encourage flowering, provided the compost is kept dry.

PROBLEM PAGES

Even the most greenfingered of indoor gardeners has a few greenfly now and again, and there are other pests and diseases that will make your life a misery. Don't worry. Take the right action promptly and your plants should soon recover. But the main causes for concern are things called physiological disorders. They're not caused by a pest or a disease but by you or your home environment. Either you're growing the plant in the wrong place, or you're doing something that upsets it.

Do your Sherlock Holmes bit to find out just what's wrong – it could be one of several things – and when you've pinpointed the culprit, take the recommended action.

Here's what might go wrong.

Leaves turning yellow If only one or two of the older leaves low down on the plant are going yellow, it's nothing more than old age or 'natural senescence'.

Plants like the weeping fig (*Ficus benjamina*) and the umbrella tree (*Heptapleurum arboricola*) will often produce a good few yellow leaves just after they've been bought and these usually fall off, too. Don't move the

Dry out an overwatered plant by standing it, minus its pot, on a wad of newspaper

plants (provided they're in a suitable spot). They'll soon recover.

If a plant has a number of leaves that are turning yellow and the above suggestions do not apply, suspect one of the following:

- Overwatering – let the compost dry out between waterings
- Shortage of light – move the plant near to a window
- Shortage of nutrients – feed the plant monthly in summer
- Draughts – move the plant

Leaves brown at the tips   Brown leaf tips show that the plant is unable to circulate sap to the extremities of the leaf due to unfavourable conditions. Guard against:

- Dry air – stand the plant on a tray of moist gravel
- Draughts – move the plant
- Scorch from a radiator – keep the plant at least 1.25m (4ft) from a heat source
- Underwatering – aim to keep the compost slightly moist but not constantly soggy

Leaves spotted with brown   Sunken brown blotches appear at random on the surface of otherwise healthy leaves. In most cases the cause will be dryness of the air around the plant due to sun scorch. If the plant sits in a brilliant window, move it to more indirect light.

Hairy-leaved plants such as African violets (saint-paulias) and gloxinias develop brown patches when water is splashed on the leaves. Avoid this by watering them from below.

If neither of these causes is to blame, suspect under-watering, or the reverse – overwatering – and take the appropriate action.

Check, the plant for any signs of pests.

Flower bud drop   Just when the buds are fattening and beginning to show colour, off they drop, never to open. The plant has received some kind of check due to one of the following circumstances:

- Dryness at the roots – keep the compost evenly moist, but not soggy, when flower buds are developing
- Dry air – stand the plant on a gravel tray in centrally heated rooms

---

Where minor pest infestations are noticed, wash the beasts off under the tap or sponge them away.

- Draughts – move the plant carefully (see below)
- Movement of the plant – Christmas cacti and fuchsias will often shed their flowers if they are moved from cool to warm temperatures, or vice-versa, while the blooms are forming
- Lack of light – move the plant into a brighter spot if it's in shade

No flowers produced The plant's obviously not in the right frame of mind to produce blooms and it's up to you to give it conditions conducive to flowering. If the plant has been overpotted (given too large a container full of fresh compost) it will probably be so busy making roots that it has no inclination to make flowers.

Alternatively, if it hasn't been fed for months it could simply be too starved to make the effort. Tomato fertiliser (diluted as instructed for tomatoes) will often coax flower-shy plants into full bloom. It's especially good on African violets (saintpaulias). If neither of these reasons apply, suspect:

- Lack of light – move the plant to a brighter spot
- Unsuitable temperatures – is the plant too warm or too cold?

Leaf fall The plant is unhappy and feels that, under the present circumstances, it hasn't the energy to keep all its leaves alive, so it sheds them. There are several reasons why this might happen:

- Overwatering – let the compost dry out between waterings
- Underwatering – try to keep the compost evenly moist, but not soggy
- Draughts – move the plant
- Sudden changes in temperature – have you recently moved the plant? Has there been a power cut? Has the weather turned warmer or colder?

Spindly shoots Plants develop long and 'drawn' shoots for one reason only – they are short of light. Plants such as pelargoniums (often called geraniums) turn pale and spindly very quickly unless kept on a sunny windowsill. Move any spindly plant into a brightly lit spot.

Stem rotting The rotting of any plant tissue is caused

Variegated plants sometimes produce plain green shoots. Snip these off as soon as they are seen.

Brown tipped yellowing leaves due to scorch and draughts

by fungus diseases, and fungus diseases only thrive in moist situations. You're keeping the plant too wet at the roots. Allow it to dry out a little between waterings – if it's not too late to save it. Dusting lightly affected areas with a fungicide powder will help to stop the rot.

Variegation fading If the brightly variegated leaves of your ivies, or umbrella tree (*Heptapleurum arboricola* 'Variegata') or any other plant are fading, the cause is almost certain to be lack of light. Move the plant to a brightly lit spot and the variegation should return.

Every now and then an otherwise healthy variegated

Mirrors can be used to increase the amount of light in a room

Don't move fuchsias, gardenias, stephanotis and Christmas cacti once the flower buds have formed or they may decide to shed the lot.

plant will throw out a plain green shoot. This is a reversion to its original form. Snip out such shoots completely and the plant should continue to produce more variegated ones.

Wilting   Leaves of healthy plants are stiff or 'turgid' due to the flow of sap in the leaves and the presence of water. If the leaves wilt it's likely that the plant is in a state of shock and unable to keep pumping round the sap with its usual vigour. It will wilt for one of several reasons:

- Overwatering – you can let the plant dry out but it will seldom recover
- Underwatering – soak the compost and the plant will usually pick up; it's always best to underwater rather than overwater
- Sun scorch – move the plant into a spot that's indirectly lit

If none of these is the case, tap the plant from its pot and look for root pests. Vine weevil grubs are the most likely cause of wilting. They are small, fat, creamy maggots which eat the roots. Precious plants that are only slightly affected can either be watered with dilute HCH, or they can have all the compost washed off their roots and be repotted carefully in sterile compost. It's better, though, to ditch any affected plant, for if the grubs spread to other house plants the results could be disastrous.

Vine weevil is an especial problem on cyclamen.

Leaves coated with white powder   When you've made sure that it's neither dust nor talcum powder you can be fairly certain that it's mildew. This is a fungus disease that attacks plant leaves. It's more prevalent in a humid atmosphere so, if possible, move the plant to a more airy room. Spray the plant with Benlate and, if the stems are overcrowded, thin them out with a pair of secateurs to improve air circulation.

Black felt-like growth on leaves   It looks dreadful but it's really quite easy to get rid of. It's called sooty mould and it's a fungus that grows on the sticky honey-dew secreted by aphids (greenfly). First of all, kill off the aphids with a specific aphicide containing a pirimi-carb. Take the plant outdoors to spray it and let the solution dry off. Now sponge off the sooty mould with a damp cloth – it will come off a glossy-leaved plant clean as a whistle and the plant will be returned to the peak of health. It's a tedious job though!

Leaves distorted and mottled Unless the variegation is a part of their attraction, plants that have mottled and twisted leaves are infected with undesirable virus diseases. There's no cure. Be hard hearted and ditch the plants in the dustbin. If they are allowed to survive the disease may spread to healthy plants. Viruses are spread by greenfly, so control the pest to control the disease.

Stems or leaves coated with grey fur It's usually during the darker months of the year, or during wet weather, that 'grey mould' appears on leaves and stems. If a leaf dies for any reason, it won't be long before this fungus disease (more properly known as botrytis) attacks it. Pelargoniums (geraniums) are often disfigured by it, especially when they are taken as cuttings – that blackening at soil level (blackleg) will soon be followed by the grey mould that looks like a fur coat.

Like all fungi, this one thrives in a humid atmosphere. Keep plants slightly drier at the roots in winter, and make sure that there's a good circulation of air around them. Pick off any leaves as soon as they start to fade, and any faded flowers, too. Plants which seem prone to the disease can be sprayed with captan.

Greenfly Everybody knows greenfly, but remember that they come in assorted colours – pink, yellow, black and brown as well as green. Spray them with a specific aphicide (an insecticide that won't kill ladybirds, bees and lacewings). Choose one based on pirimicarb.

If you're inclined to be soft-hearted and leave greenfly alone, think again – they weaken the plant by sucking its sap, they transmit crippling virus diseases, and they secrete sticky honeydew that is rapidly colonised by sooty mould. It's not worth having them. If you hate insecticides, brush the bugs off the plant at regular intervals with a dry paint brush, but they'll rapidly return.

Whitefly Unlike greenfly, which only take off when they've exhausted their food supply, whitefly have wings which they use regularly. Tap the leaf and those miniature Concorde-shaped flies will zoom around in circles. They affect the plant in exactly the same way as greenfly but are rather more difficult to kill off because the youngsters are tiny scales that seem immune to most insecticides. Spray with bioresmethrin and repeat the application as recommended on the bottle to control adults which will emerge from the resistant scales. Two or three sprays may be necessary to effect a complete control.

Scale insects   These are the barnacles of the plant pest world. They cling to the stems and leaves, especially on glossy-leaved plants such as orange plants and bird's nest ferns (*Asplenium nidus*). They look like tiny brown limpets. Dab them with a paintbrush dipped in methylated spirits, or spray the plant with malathion. The trouble is that ferns are very sensitive to chemicals and you'd be well advised to gently wash the scales off them with damp cottonwool. They suck sap and secrete honeydew just like aphids.

Mealy bugs   These are closely related to scale insects

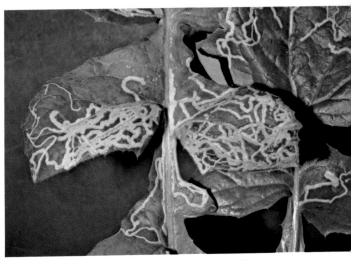

Leaf miner damage on chrysanthemum – see page 58

Oranges and lemons can be grown from pips but may take seven or eight years to flower and produce fruits (small ones!).

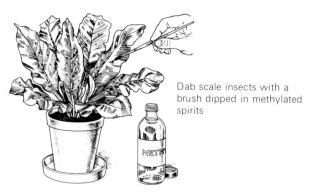

Dab scale insects with a brush dipped in methylated spirits

and are just as tricky to control. They do move (but very slowly) and are coated in a white, waxy wool. They usually colonise leaf axils and other nooks and crannies. Treat them the same as scale insects.

Red spider mites   No. These are not those tiny red spiders you see running about on windowsills. Red spider mites are, for a start, brown or yellowish in colour and about the size of a pin-prick. They colonise plants in a dry atmosphere, sucking sap and bleaching the foliage so that it becomes yellowish and crisp. Examine the undersides of the leaf and you'll find masses of minute specks running around. In severe outbreaks tiny webs are spun over the leaves.

These mites are discouraged by a moist atmosphere, so prevent attacks by standing susceptible plants on trays of moist gravel. Spraying the foliage with tepid water also helps prevent their establishment. Spray any outbreaks with systemic insecticides – varying the product from time to time so that the pest doesn't build up a resistance.

Leaf miners   These are the pests that cause those little white ribbon-like scars to be produced on the leaves of chrysanthemums and cinerarias (senecio). The scars are actually tunnels made by the grub which chews its way between the upper and lower leaf surfaces. Pick off badly infected leaves and spray the plant with fenitrothion.

Vine weevils (See wilting, page 55).   In minor attacks, the pot can be watered with a dilute solution of HCH. Otherwise, the dustbin is the best place for the casualty.

Variegated plants usually need brighter light than plants with plain green leaves.

SAFETY

Whenever you're using a chemical to exterminate a pest or disease, do remember to store it out of the reach of children in a properly labelled container. Use it strictly in accordance with the manufacturer's instructions, and spray your house plants *outdoors*. Make sure you use the right product for the job. Dispose of any excess chemical mixtures down the lavatory. Thoroughly rinse out all hand sprayers after use, and store them safely.

INDEX

ALL ABOUT HOUSE PLANTS